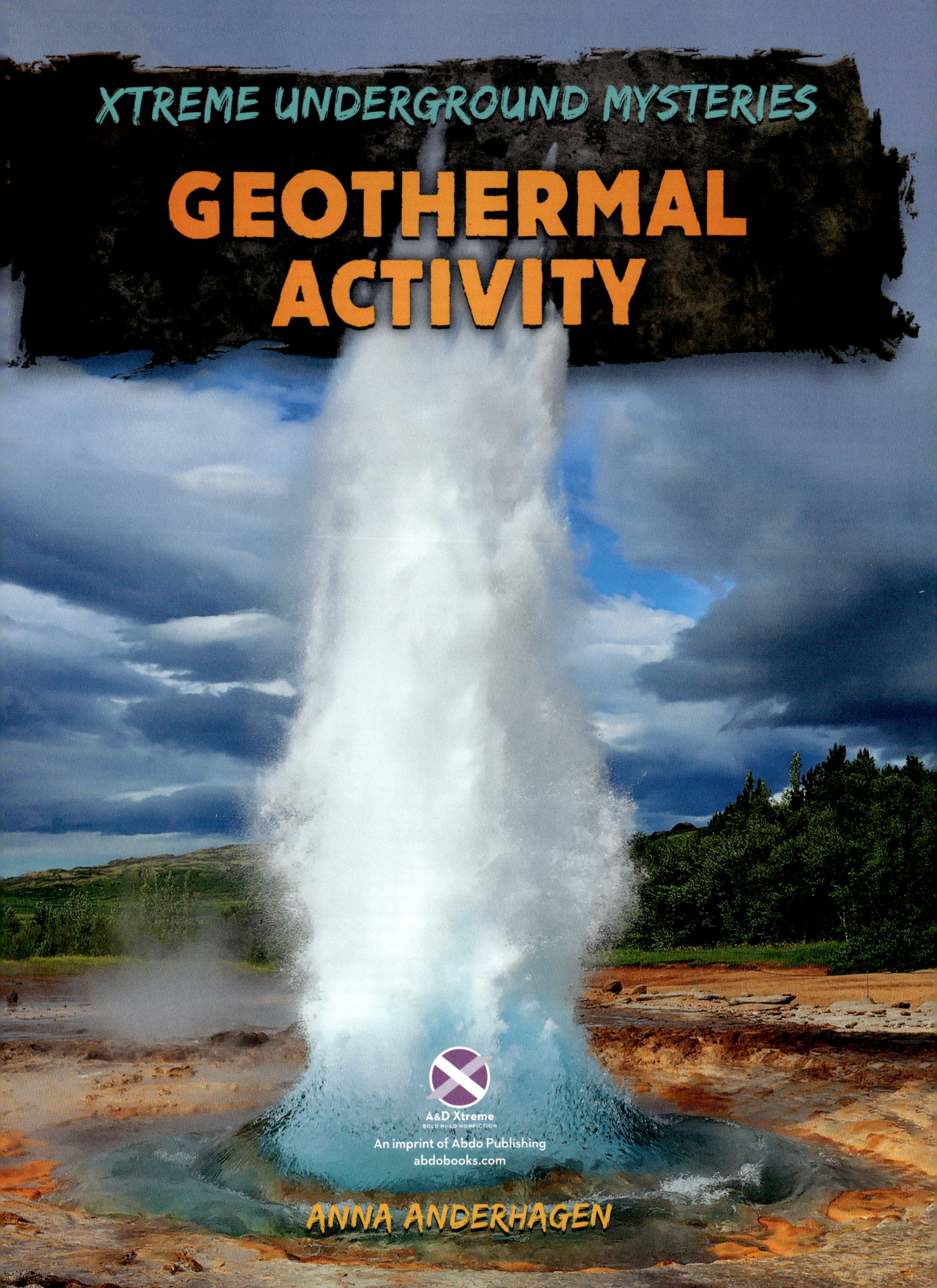
XTREME UNDERGROUND MYSTERIES
GEOTHERMAL ACTIVITY
A&D Xtreme
An imprint of Abdo Publishing
abdobooks.com
ANNA ANDERHAGEN

TAKE IT TO THE XTREME!

GET READY FOR AN EXTREME ADVENTURE!
THE PAGES OF THIS BOOK WILL TAKE YOU INTO
THE WONDROUS WORLD BENEATH YOUR FEET.
WHEN YOU HAVE FINISHED READING THIS BOOK, TAKE THE
XTREME CHALLENGE ON PAGE 45 ABOUT WHAT YOU'VE LEARNED!

ABDOBOOKS.COM
Published by Abdo Publishing, a division of ABDO, PO Box 398166, Minneapolis, Minnesota 55439.
Copyright © 2026 by Abdo Consulting Group, Inc. International copyrights reserved in all countries. No part of this book may be reproduced in any form without written permission from the publisher.
A&D Xtreme™ is a trademark and logo of Abdo Publishing.
Printed in the United States of America, North Mankato, MN.
102025
012026

Design: Kelly Doudna, Mighty Media, Inc.
Production: Mighty Media, Inc.
Editor: Katherine Chu

Cover Photograph: kavram/Shutterstock
Interior Photographs: alfotokunst/Adobe Stock, pp. 20–21; Arman Ogandzhanyan/Shutterstock, pp. 40–41; Bob/Adobe Stock, pp. 26–27; boyloso/Adobe Stock, pp. 28–29; CherylRamalho/Shutterstock, pp. 4–5; Dave Bunnell/Under Earth Images/Wikimedia Commons, p. 39; Diana/Adobe Stock, pp. 22–23; Dmitry Pichugin/Adobe Stock, pp. 24–25; f11photo/Shutterstock, pp. 14–15; GenadijsZ/Shutterstock, pp. 32–33; Helena Bilkova/Adobe Stock, pp. 10–11; imageBROKER.com/Shutterstock, pp. 18–19; jeanmi/Adobe Stock, p. 44; Jeffrey Judd/USGS, pp. 42–43; kavram/Shutterstock, p. 1; Kevin L Bishop/Adobe Stock, pp. 38–39; KRIS WIKTOR/Adobe Stock, pp. 8–9; Matej Hudovernik/Shutterstock, pp. 34–35; Mateusz Nowak/Adobe Stock, pp. 16–17; NPS/Wikimedia Commons, p. 13; Shu-Hung Liu/Shutterstock, pp. 12–13; USGS, p. 42; Vadim Nefedov/Adobe Stock, pp. 36–37; Veniamin Zhuravlov/Adobe Stock, pp. 6–7; WitR/Shutterstock, pp. 30–31
Design Elements: tsayuet/Adobe Stock (rocky texture); Tunatura/Adobe Stock (tunnel texture)

LIBRARY OF CONGRESS CONTROL NUMBER: 2025939218
PUBLISHER'S CATALOGING-IN-PUBLICATION DATA
Names: Anderhagen, Anna, author.
Title: Geothermal activity / by Anna Anderhagen
Description: Minneapolis, Minnesota : Abdo Publishing, 2026 | Series: Xtreme underground mysteries | Includes online resources and index.
Identifiers: ISBN 9781098297800 (lib. bdg.) | ISBN 9798384930617 (ebook)
Subjects: LCSH: Geothermal energy--Juvenile literature. | Thermal waters--Juvenile literature. | Energy systems--Juvenile literature. | Geosciences--Juvenile literature. | Earth sciences--Juvenile literature.
Classification: DDC 551.2--dc23

CONTENTS

CHAPTER 1

HISS, BUBBLE, POP!

Yellowstone has the most geysers, hot springs, steam vents, and mud pots on Earth!

Shoshone hunters were tracking a bison herd in what is now Yellowstone. They passed a nearby hot spring that spat steam with a hiss. Boiling water bubbled and popped. Suddenly, a burst of water shot into the sky with a roar. The Shoshone had just seen a geyser!

CHAPTER 2

MYSTERIOUS EVENTS

Magma is partly melted rock below Earth's surface. It heats surrounding water and rocks. This causes geothermal events such as geysers, hot springs, mud pots, **fumaroles**, **volcanoes**, and more.

Geothermal events happen in places where Earth's heat escapes through cracks in the ground. The events produce geothermal energy. Geothermal energy is the heat made within Earth.

Lava is magma that breaks through Earth's surface.

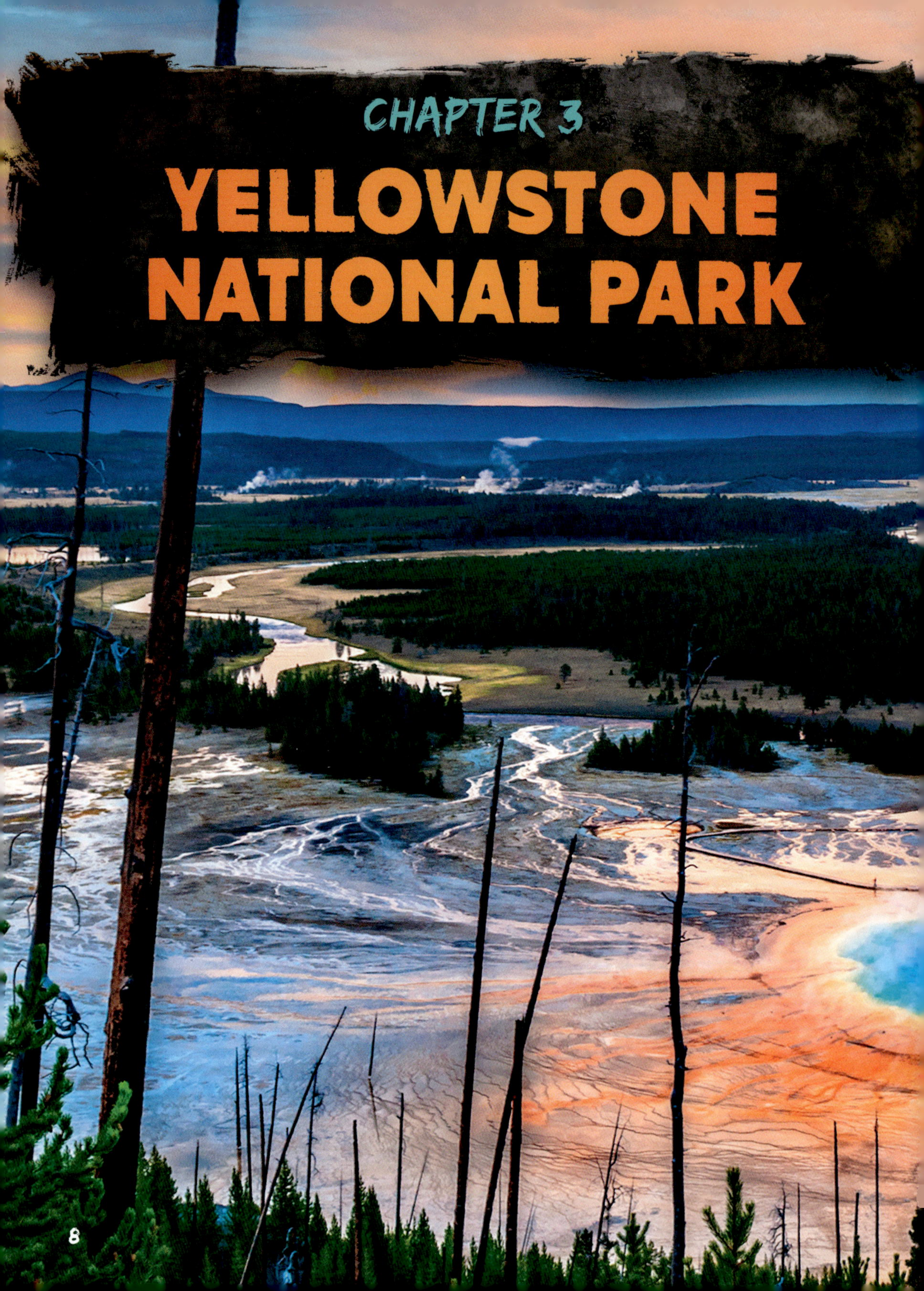

CHAPTER 3
YELLOWSTONE NATIONAL PARK

Yellowstone National Park is mostly in Wyoming. The park rests on a huge underground **volcano**. It has more than 10,000 geothermal features. These include geysers, mud pots, hot springs, and **fumaroles**.

Yellowstone's geothermal features have been active for more than two million years.

Old Faithful is Yellowstone's most famous geyser. It shoots boiling water more than 100 feet (30 m) in the air every 91 minutes.

Magma lies about four to six miles (6 to 10 km) beneath Yellowstone. It heats water deep underground. The hot water rises and bursts through Earth's surface as geysers.

XTREME FACT

Yellowstone holds about half of the world's geysers.

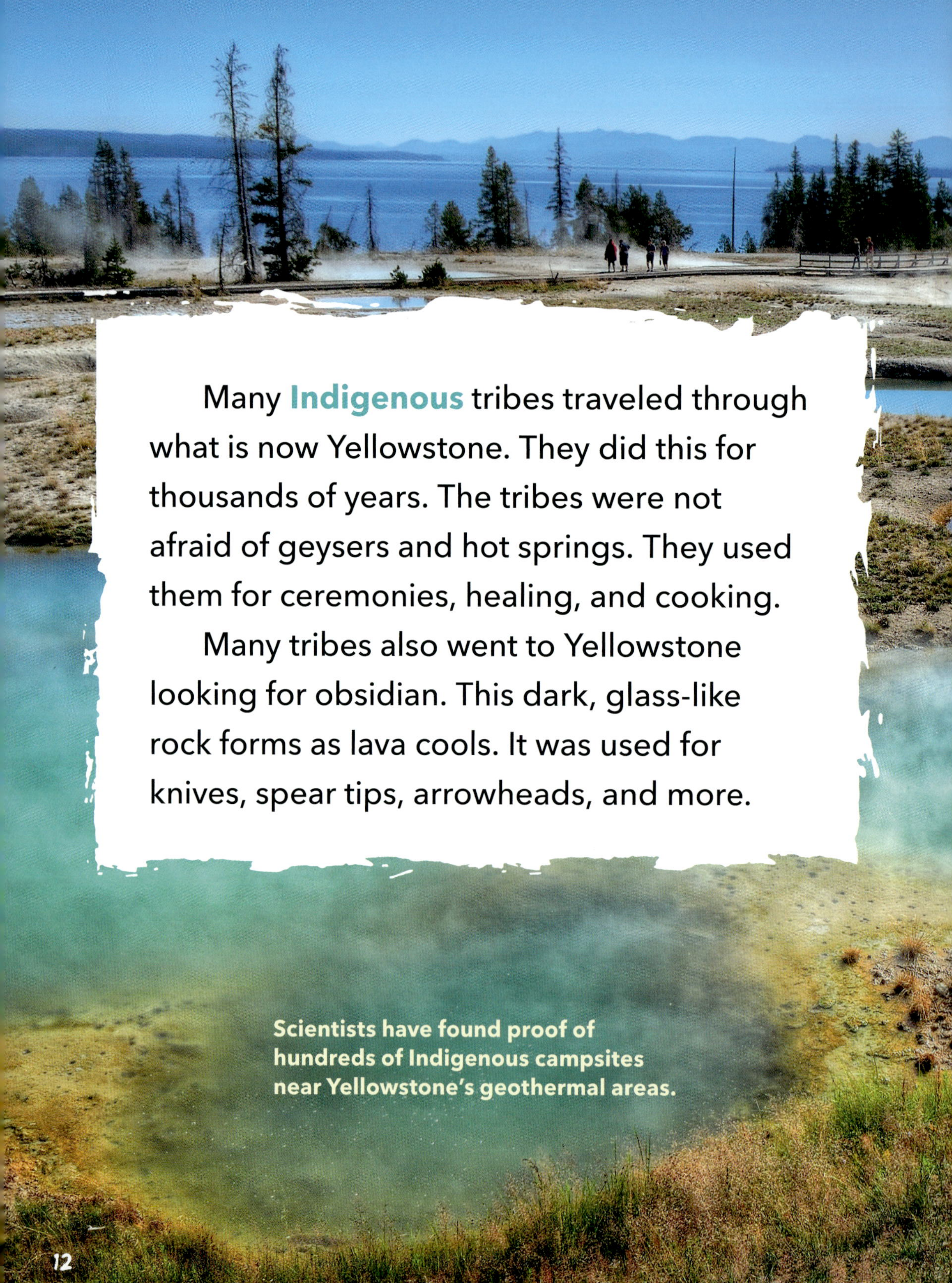

Many **Indigenous** tribes traveled through what is now Yellowstone. They did this for thousands of years. The tribes were not afraid of geysers and hot springs. They used them for ceremonies, healing, and cooking.

Many tribes also went to Yellowstone looking for obsidian. This dark, glass-like rock forms as lava cools. It was used for knives, spear tips, arrowheads, and more.

Scientists have found proof of hundreds of Indigenous campsites near Yellowstone's geothermal areas.

A blade created from Yellowstone's obsidian

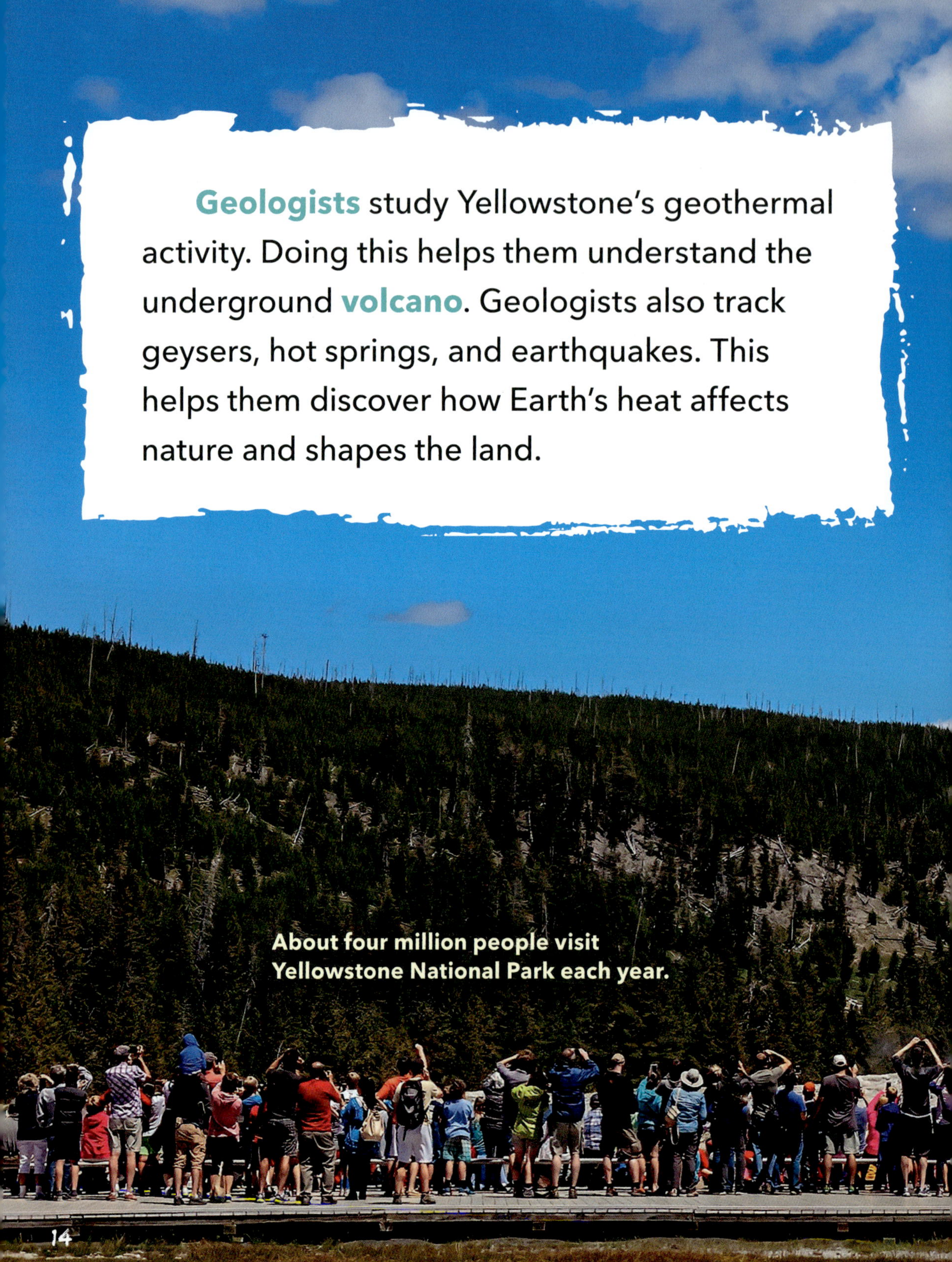

Geologists study Yellowstone's geothermal activity. Doing this helps them understand the underground **volcano**. Geologists also track geysers, hot springs, and earthquakes. This helps them discover how Earth's heat affects nature and shapes the land.

About four million people visit Yellowstone National Park each year.

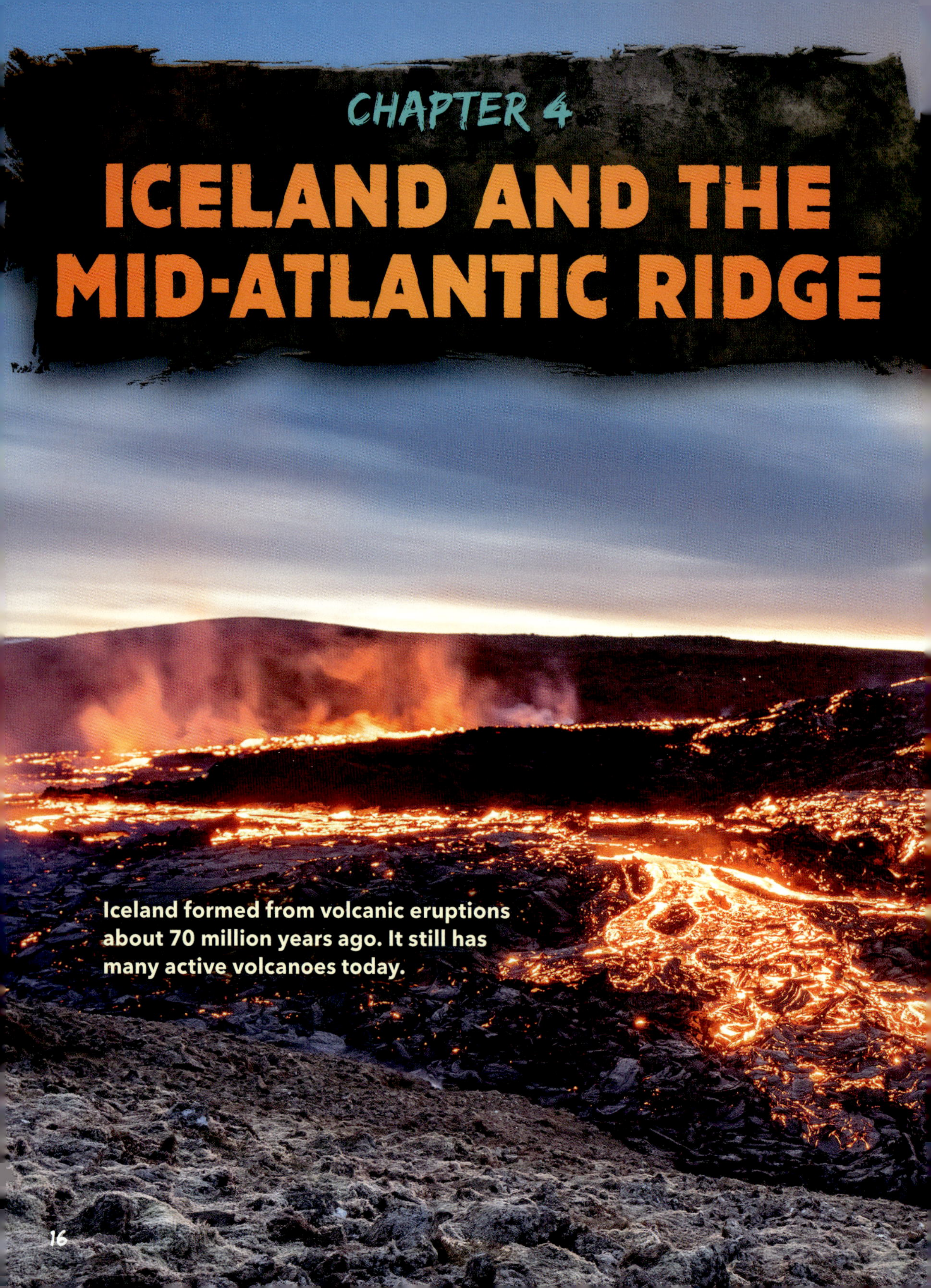

CHAPTER 4

ICELAND AND THE MID-ATLANTIC RIDGE

Iceland formed from volcanic eruptions about 70 million years ago. It still has many active volcanoes today.

Iceland sits on the Mid-Atlantic Ridge. This is where two **tectonic plates** move apart. Magma seeps through the gaps. It heats underground water, or groundwater. The groundwater rises to the surface. It creates Iceland's hot springs, geysers, and **fumaroles**.

One of Iceland's most popular hot springs is the Blue Lagoon. Heated groundwater rises to the surface. As it does, it collects **minerals** from the ground. These minerals mix with **algae** and other organisms in the hot spring. This gives the Blue Lagoon its famous blue color.

XTREME FACT

Icelanders use hot springs to bathe, cook, and wash clothes.

The Blue Lagoon was created next to a geothermal power plant in 1976. More than 700,000 people visit it every year for its health benefits.

XTREME FACT

Icelanders use heat and steam from hot springs to make Icelandic bread called *rúgbrauð*.

About 66 percent of homes in Iceland use geothermal energy.

Iceland has seven geothermal power plants. The power plants pump hot water from underground. The hot water's steam turns **rotors** in special machines. This creates electricity!

Geologists and **geochemists** study Iceland's hot springs. They test the water temperature, **minerals**, and bacteria levels. This helps them learn how hot springs form.

Scientists also explore how underground heat affects water, rocks, and **microorganisms**. And they study how people use hot springs for energy and health benefits.

Iceland has more than 45 hot springs. The hottest is Deildartunguhver. It can reach 212 degrees Fahrenheit (100°C)!

CHAPTER 5

ROTORUA, NEW ZEALAND

Rotorua is in New Zealand's Taupō **Volcanic** Zone. It sits inside the crater of a **dormant** volcano. The volcano erupted more than 280,000 years ago. Magma continues to heat groundwater, making the water hot and creating steam. This creates hot bubbling mud pots, **fumaroles**, and geysers.

The Lady Knox Geyser at Wai-O-Tapu, Rotorua, erupts at 10:15 a.m. every day.

XTREME FACT

Hell's Gate is a spa in Rotorua. It offers mud pot baths. But the mud is very hot. So, people can only stay in the bath for 20 minutes.

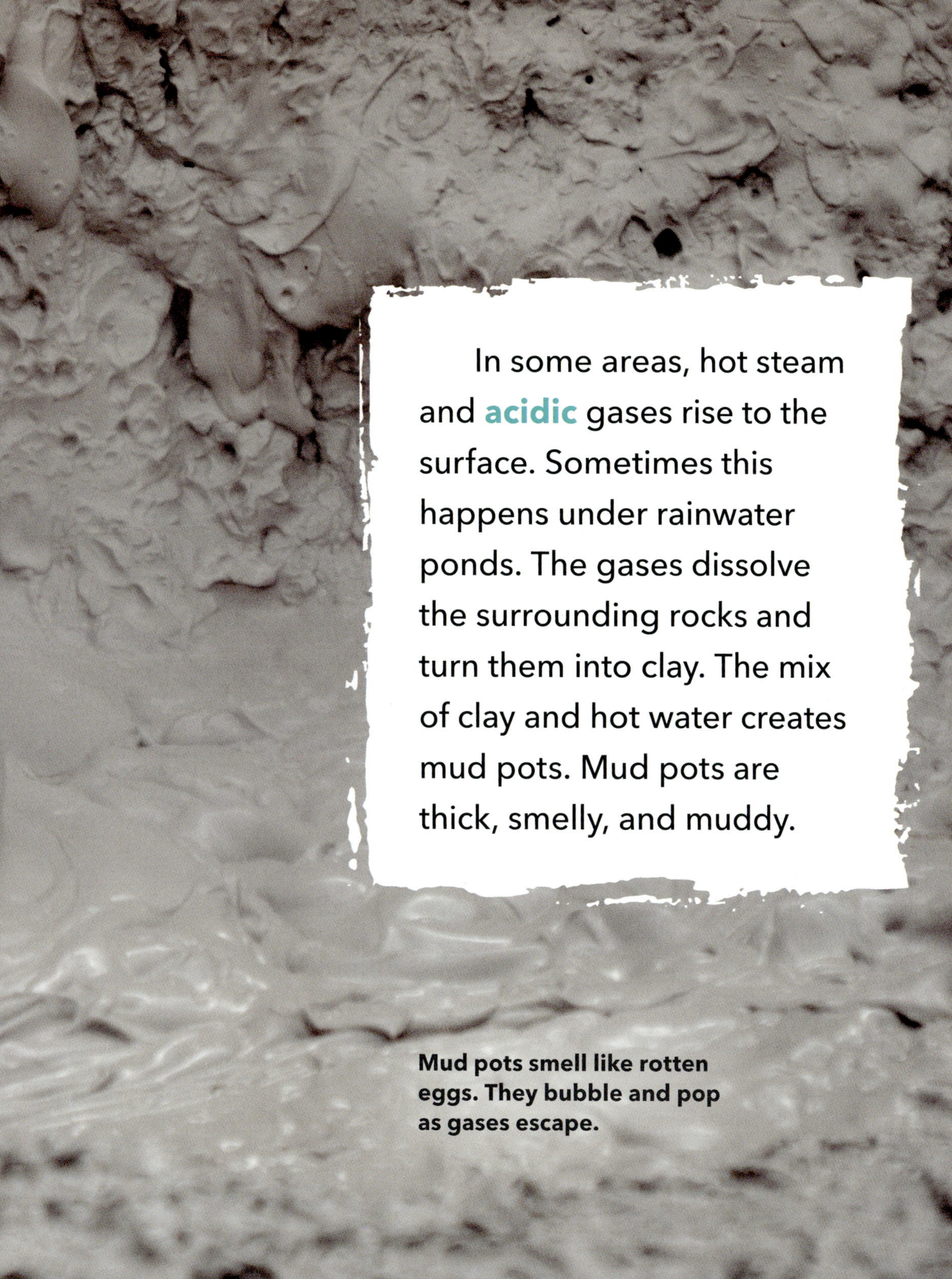

In some areas, hot steam and **acidic** gases rise to the surface. Sometimes this happens under rainwater ponds. The gases dissolve the surrounding rocks and turn them into clay. The mix of clay and hot water creates mud pots. Mud pots are thick, smelly, and muddy.

Mud pots smell like rotten eggs. They bubble and pop as gases escape.

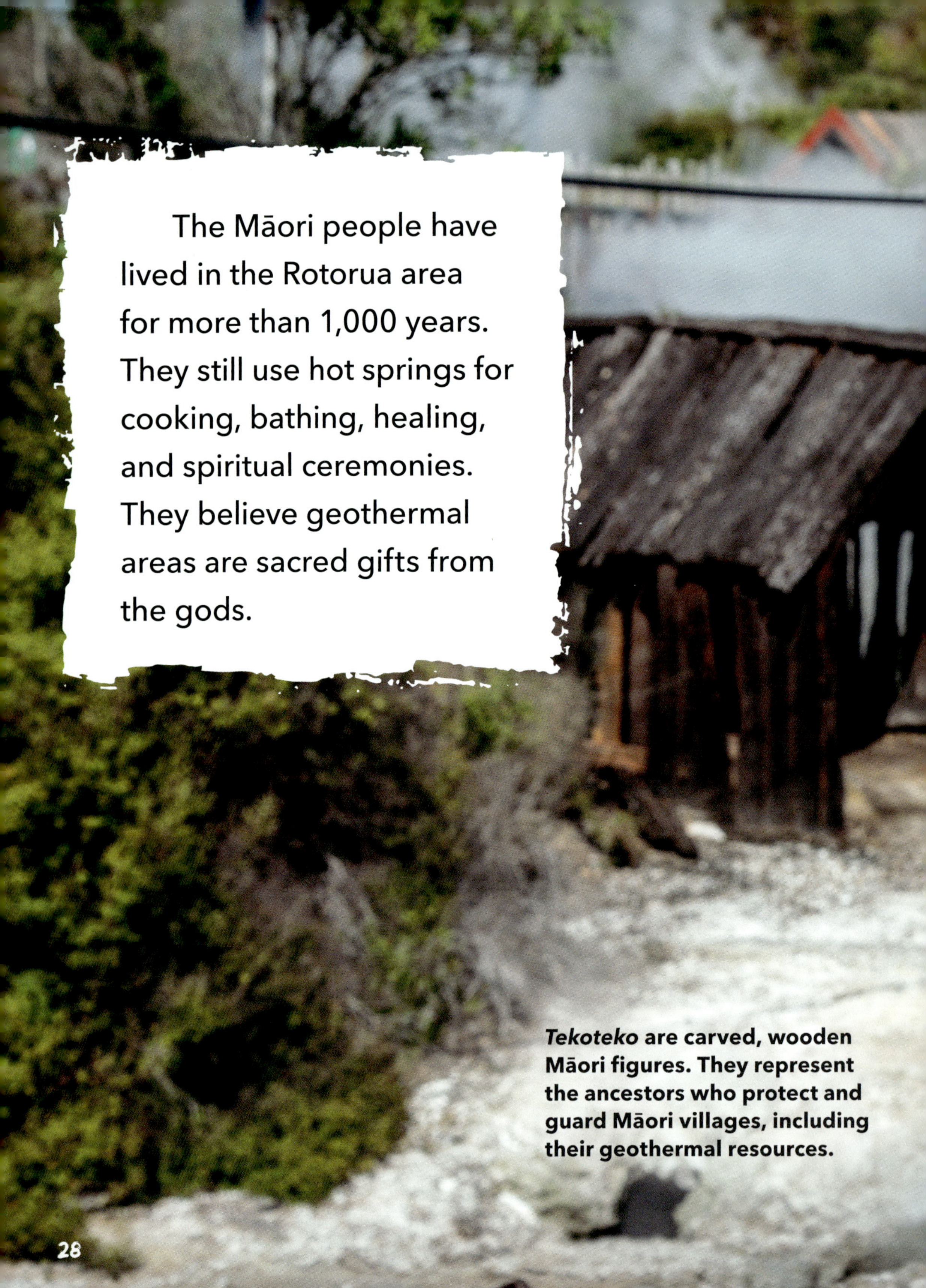

The Māori people have lived in the Rotorua area for more than 1,000 years. They still use hot springs for cooking, bathing, healing, and spiritual ceremonies. They believe geothermal areas are sacred gifts from the gods.

***Tekoteko* are carved, wooden Māori figures. They represent the ancestors who protect and guard Māori villages, including their geothermal resources.**

More than three million people visit Rotorua's geothermal sites each year.

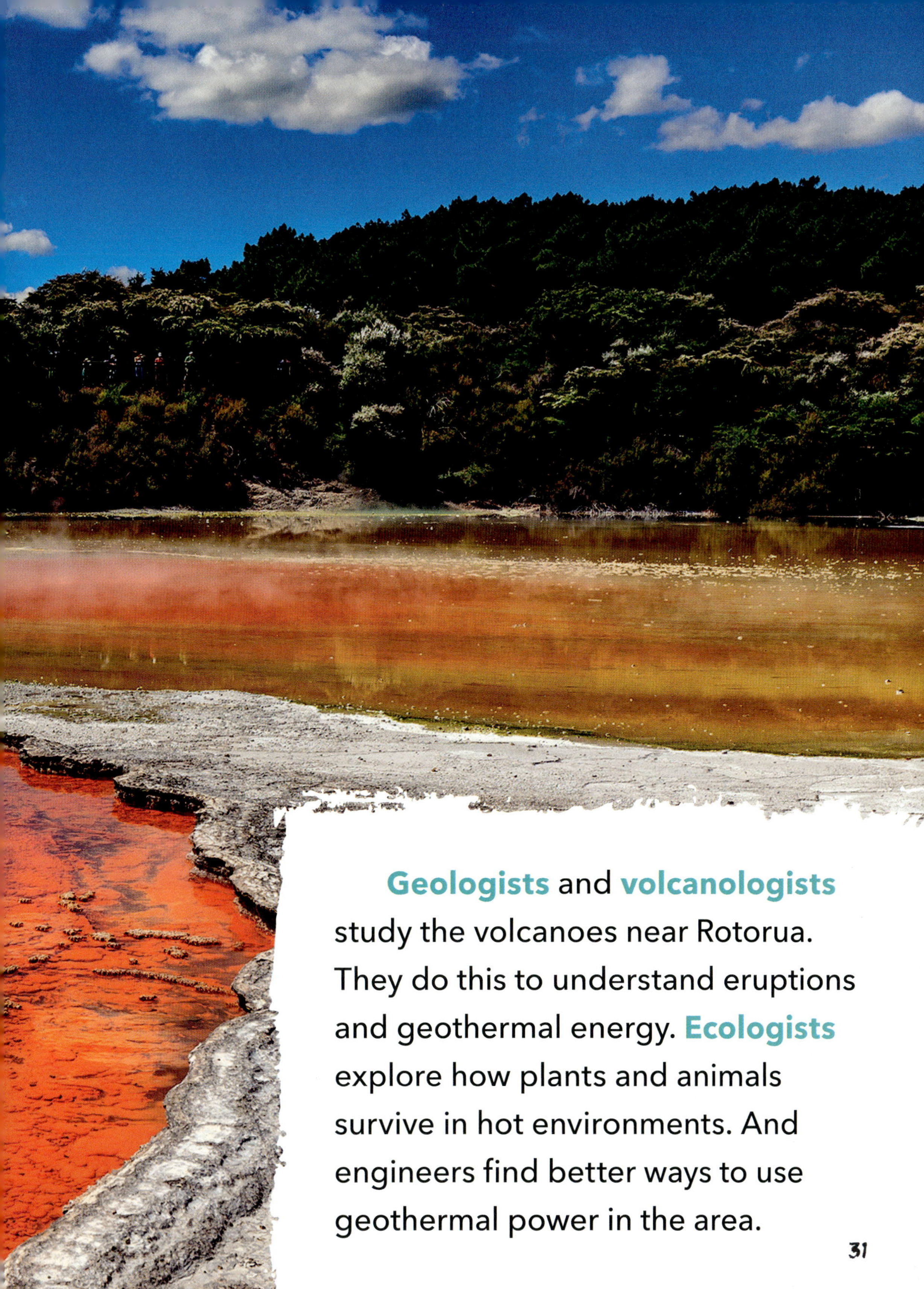

Geologists and **volcanologists** study the volcanoes near Rotorua. They do this to understand eruptions and geothermal energy. **Ecologists** explore how plants and animals survive in hot environments. And engineers find better ways to use geothermal power in the area.

CHAPTER 6

DALLOL, ETHIOPIA

Dallol is in the Danakil **Depression**, which is part of the Afar Triangle. The Afar Triangle is an area where three **tectonic plates** pull apart. The movement forms cracks in the ground. Heat, water, and gas escape from these cracks. This creates **acidic** springs, geysers, and **fumaroles**.

Dallol is one of the hottest places on Earth. Temperatures can reach about 130 degrees Fahrenheit (54°C)!

XTREME FACT

Dallol's geothermal system has been active for at least 6,000 years.

XTREME FACT

Fumaroles can vent deadly gases. These include sulfur dioxide, hydrogen sulfide, hydrogen chloride, and more.

In Dallol, steam and gas escape through **fumaroles**. Fumaroles hiss, sizzle, crack, and sometimes smell like rotten eggs. They can let out steam and gas for hundreds of years. Fumaroles can also quickly disappear if their heat source cools down.

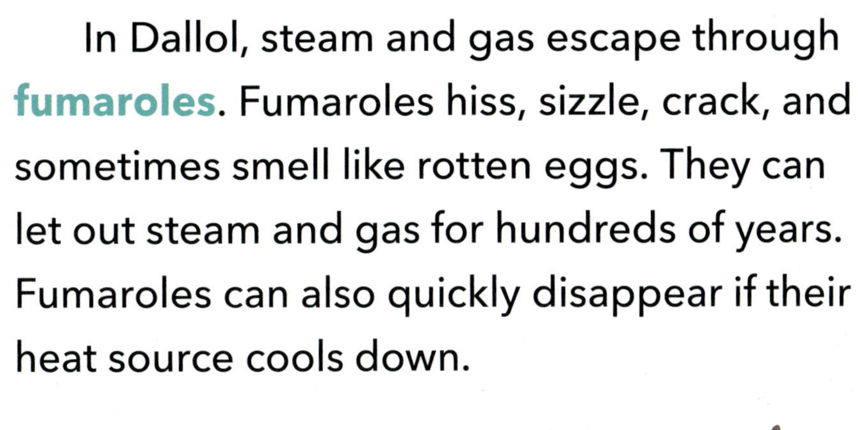

The water in fumaroles reaches more than 200 degrees Fahrenheit (93°C) and is often acidic. The environment is also very salty.

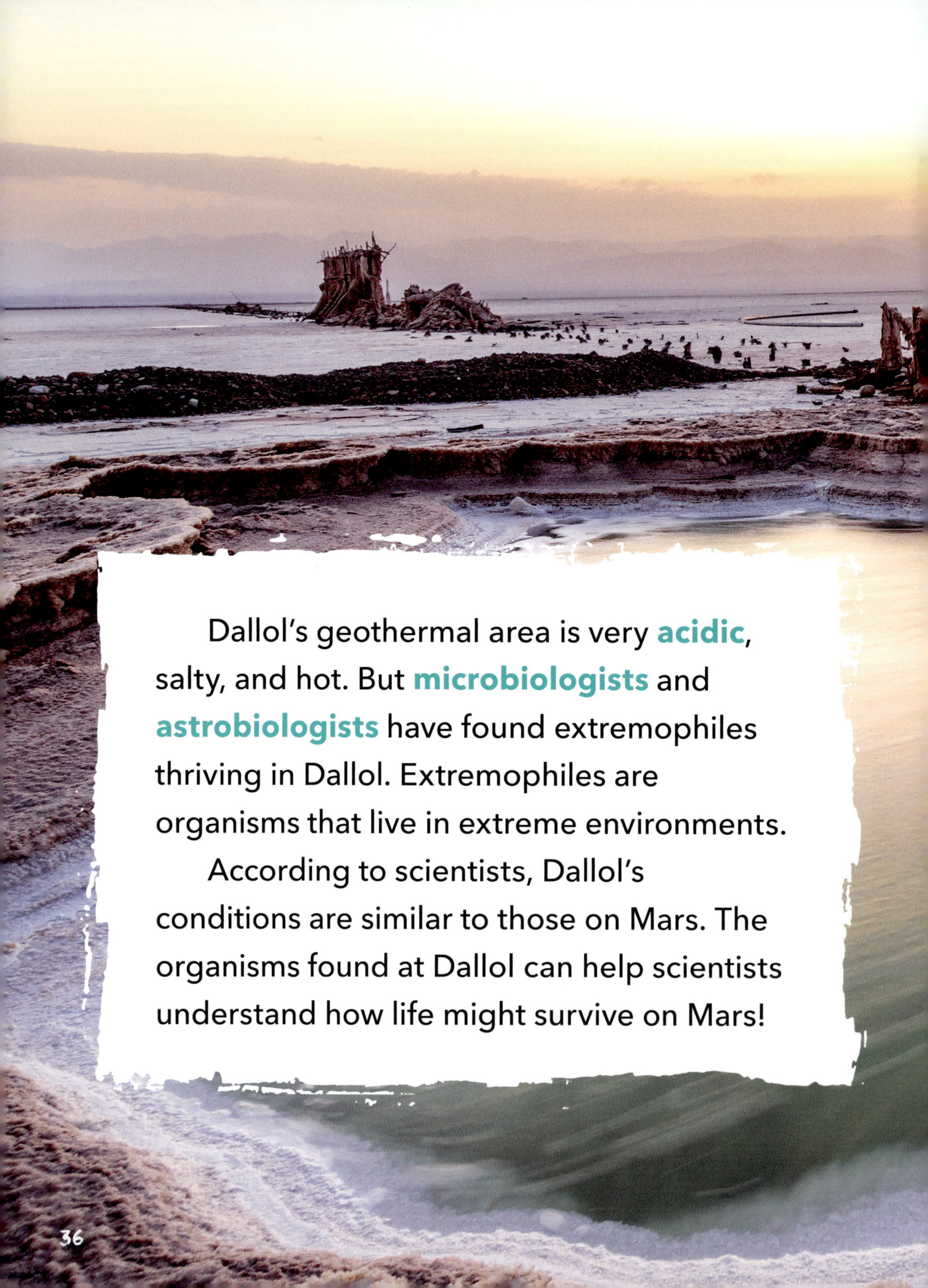

Dallol's geothermal area is very **acidic**, salty, and hot. But **microbiologists** and **astrobiologists** have found extremophiles thriving in Dallol. Extremophiles are organisms that live in extreme environments.

According to scientists, Dallol's conditions are similar to those on Mars. The organisms found at Dallol can help scientists understand how life might survive on Mars!

An abandoned salt mining settlement near Dallol. The Afar people have lived in this hot environment for thousands of years. They still mine the salt in the area.

CHAPTER 7
HAWAII'S LAVA TUBES

The Kīlauea Volcano is one of Earth's most active volcanoes.

The Kazumura lava tube system is in Hawaii. It formed when the Kīlauea **Volcano** erupted in the 1400s. The lava's outer layer cooled and hardened as it flowed. After the eruption, the remaining lava drained out. This left a long tunnel, or lava tube.

The Kazumura lava tube system is the longest lava tube cave in the world. It's more than 40 miles (65 km) long.

Nāhuku is also known as the Thurston Lava Tube. It is one of Hawaii's most visited lava tubes.

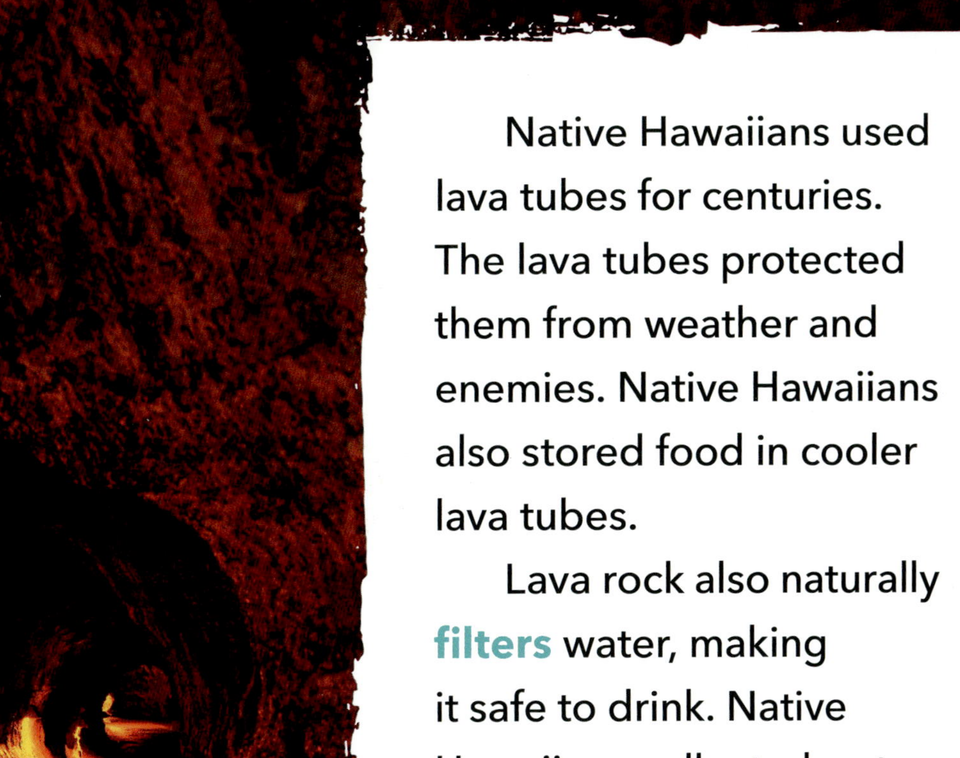

Native Hawaiians used lava tubes for centuries. The lava tubes protected them from weather and enemies. Native Hawaiians also stored food in cooler lava tubes.

Lava rock also naturally **filters** water, making it safe to drink. Native Hawaiians collected water as it dripped from lava tube ceilings. They also held ceremonies and buried important people in lava tubes.

Lava flows through an active lava tube at temperatures of more than 2,000 degrees Fahrenheit (1,090°C)!

Geologists study lava tubes. Lava tubes help them learn about **volcanoes** and Earth's history. Scientists also use lava tubes to study how future astronauts might live on the moon. There are many pits on the moon. These pits could lead to huge caves, similar to the lava tubes on Earth!

Kīlauea Volcano erupts in 2018. Eruptions like this lead to active lava tubes.

CHAPTER 8

WHAT IS HIDING UNDER YOUR FEET?

Scientists may soon discover new magma chambers, extreme life-forms, and geothermal energy sources. They may also learn more about how geothermal activity affects Earth's climate and **ecosystems**. The ground beneath our feet is full of mysteries just waiting to be explored!

Scientists believe Dallol's bright colors are created by the mix of different gases and salt.

XTREME CHALLENGE

TAKE THE QUIZ BELOW AND PUT WHAT YOU'VE LEARNED TO THE TEST!

1) What is geothermal activity?

2) What are some examples of geothermal events?

3) Where would you like to visit to see geothermal activity?

4) Why do you think people visit Yellowstone, Iceland, and Rotorua to see geysers?

GLOSSARY

acidic–containing a type of chemical that reacts when mixed with a base.

algae–plants or tiny plantlike organisms that live mainly in water.

astrobiologist–a scientist who investigates whether life could exist beyond Earth. To do this, they study life, nature, and outer space.

depression–an area that is lower than the area surrounding it.

dormant–asleep, or not active.

ecologist–a scientist who studies how living things interact with each other and their environment.

ecosystem–a community of organisms and their surroundings.

filter–to remove solid pieces from a liquid or gas.

fumarole–a crack or hole in the ground where hot steam and gas escape from inside the earth.

geochemist–a scientist who studies Earth's composition, processes, structures, and other physical features to understand how they work.

geologist–a person who studies the science of Earth and its structure.

Indigenous–native to a certain place.

microbiologist–a scientist who studies small life-forms.

microorganism–a living thing that is too small to see with the naked eye.

mineral—a natural substance that makes up rocks and other parts of nature.

rotor—a part in a machine that rotates, or turns, inside another part.

Shoshone—an Indigenous people who live in California, Nevada, Utah, Idaho, and Wyoming.

tectonic plates—huge, slow-moving pieces of Earth's crust that float on top of the softer layer below. They cause earthquakes, volcanoes, and the creation of mountains.

volcano—a deep opening in Earth's surface from which hot liquid rock or steam comes out. A volcanologist is a scientist who studies volcanoes. Something that relates to volcanoes is volcanic.

ONLINE RESOURCES

To learn more about geothermal activity, please visit **abdobooklinks.com** or scan this QR code. These links are routinely monitored and updated to provide the most current information available.

INDEX